AF483837

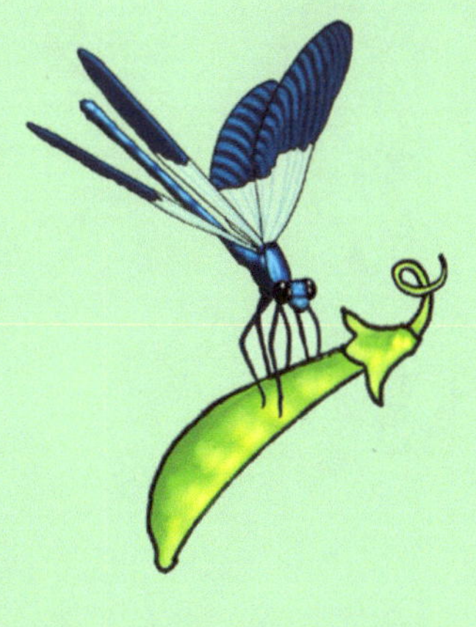

ABC
Come Garden with Me

Jane Bosko
&
Painted Grace

To my three Es
Emberley, Easton and Ender
I love you so much

Scavenger Hunt
Can You Find Them All?

(1) Dragonfly 

(4) Beetles 

(26) Butterflies 

(8) Bees 

(4) Ants 

(15) Ladybugs 

(8) Snails 

THE SUN IS OUT, THE BIRDS ARE CHIRPING.
IN THE GARDEN, IT'S TIME TO START WORKING.
THE GROUND IS SOFT, THE AIR IS WARM,
TIME TO GET THIS GARDEN ADORNED.
WE PULL UP THE WEEDS AND GATHER OUR SEEDS,
OH I HOPE WE DO SUCCEED!

FOLLOW ME AS I PLANT
EACH ROW.
FROM A TO Z WE SHALL SOW;
WITH EACH LETTER THERE IS
SOMETHING NEW
TO GROW.

ASPARAGUS

LET'S START WITH A HEALTHY GREEN
ASPARAGUS IS WHAT I MEAN!

Asparagus

Basil

This next one is always a true winner.
Soon we will have my favorite
Basil Pesto dinner!

Basil

CHAMOMILE

THESE SMALL WHITE FLOWERS
SMELL SO SWEET,
WITH HOT WATER AND HONEY
THEY CERTAINLY WILL MAKE
A TREAT.

Chamomile
Basil

DANDELION
DANDELIONS MIGHT BE A WEED
BUT THEIR BRIGHT COLORED FLOWERS
ARE JUST WHAT WE NEED.

ENDIVE
ENDIVE HAS ALWAYS BEEN A
FAVORITE OF MINE,
ESPECIALLY ROASTED,
AND SPRINKLED WITH THYME!
Endive

FENUGREEK
THIS NEXT ONE IS SURE TO CHEER YOU UP
IT'S GROWN IN EASTERN EUROPE
AND SMELLS LIKE MAPLE SYRUP.

GOURDS

GOURDS WILL BE READY
BIG AND SMALL;
JUST IN TIME
FOR WHEN THE LEAVES
START TO FALL.

HOLLYHOCK
TALL STALKS OF HOLLYHOCK
ARE SURE TO BRING A FLOCK
(of BUTTERFLIES!)

ICEPLANT

WE RECENTLY DISCOVERED THIS
BEAUTIFUL GROUND COVER.
ICEPLANT IS SIMPLY NOT
LIKE ANY OTHER!

Jasmine

These fragrant
little stars of Jasmine
are as white as the mountain tops
in Aspen.

KALE

WE ALWAYS MAKES SURE TO
PLANT EXTRA KALE,
SO WE CAN LEAVE A FEW STALKS
FOR THE SNAILS!

Kale

LEEK

THIS NEXT ONE TAKES
ABOUT TWENTY WEEKS;
FROM SEED TO SPROUT
TO GIANT LEEKS!

MINT

THERE IS NOTHING AS SWEET, COOL
AND REFRESHING AS MINT.
IT WILL CERTAINLY GROW IN A
SPRINT!

Mint

Mint

Nasturtium

Orange, yellow and red Nasturtiums will look beautiful in this garden bed.

ONION

ONIONS ARE A MUST
IN EVERY GARDEN.
FROM WHITE TO YELLOW
TO GREEN,
I JUST CANT WAIT UNTIL THEY
ARE SEEN!

Onion

PEA

PEAS GROW IN PODS
ON LONG, LONG VINES
SO, SOMETIMES WE NEED
A LITTLE TWINE.

Asparagus

Quinoa

Sweet, nutty and high in protein
Quinoa's colors make
a beautiful scene.

Rosemary

THIS HERB SMELLS OF EVERGREEN
WITH PINK AND PURPLE FLOWERS
SHE'LL BE LOOKING LIKE A QUEEN!
Rosemary

SUNFLOWER

LET'S PLANT THESE
BIG BEAUTIFUL BLOOMS
TO GIVE US SOME SHADE
AS THEIR TOWERS WILL LOOM.

 Thyme

These tiny green leaves,
with a rich earthy taste,
are one of my favorite herbs,
and it doesn't need much space!

UPRIGHT CLEMATIS

IT WILL STAND TALL
WITHOUT A LATTICE;
IN THE GARDEN IT'S SURE TO
MAKE A STATUS.

VERVAIN

VERVAIN'S FLOWERS OF
PURPLE AND PINK,
ATTRACT BUTTERFLIES
IN A WINK!

WATERMELON

Watermelons grow on vines.
In the summer time
they are sure to shine!

Xyris

Xyris is a yellow-eyed grass.
It surely will give this bed
some contrast.

YARROW
Onion
Leek
YARROW HAS UMBRELLA-SHAPED FLOWERS, WHICH WILL COME IN HANDY DURING THE NEXT RAIN SHOWER!

ZINNIA
ZINNIAS COME IN A VARIETY OF COLORS,
WHEN PUT TOGETHER,
THEY MAKE A PERFECT BOUQUET
FOR MY MOTHER!